Eating Right

by Helen Frost

Consulting Editor: Gail Saunders-Smith, Ph.D.

Consultant: Linda Hathaway
Health Educator
McMillen Center for Health Education

Pebble Books

an imprint of Capstone Press
Mankato, Minnesota

Pebble Books are published by Capstone Press
151 Good Counsel Drive, P.O. Box 669, Mankato, Minnesota 56002
http://www.capstone-press.com

1 2 3 4 5 6 05 04 03 02 01 00

Library of Congress Cataloging-in-Publication Data
Frost, Helen, 1949–
    Eating right/by Helen Frost.
    p. cm.—(The food guide pyramid)
    Includes bibliographical references and index.
    Summary: Simple text and photographs describe the food guide pyramid and
show examples of food in each group.
    ISBN 0-7368-0535-4
    1. Nutrition—Juvenile literature. 2. Health—Juvenile literature. 3. Food—
Health aspects—Juvenile literature. [1. Nutrition. 2. Health. 3. Food.] I. Title.
II. Series.
RA784 .F765 2000
613.2—dc21   99-054933

Note to Parents and Teachers

The Food Guide Pyramid series supports national science standards
related to physical health and nutrition. This book describes and
illustrates the food groups of the food guide pyramid. The
photographs support early readers in understanding the text. The
repetition of words and phrases helps early readers learn new
words. This book also introduces early readers to subject-specific
vocabulary words, which are defined in the Words to Know section.
Early readers may need assistance to read some words and to use
the Table of Contents, Words to Know, Read More, Internet Sites,
and Index/Word List sections of the book.

Table of Contents

The Food Guide Pyramid 5
Food Groups 9
Healthy Food Choices 21

Words to Know 22
Read More 23
Internet Sites 23
Index/Word List 24

4

You need to eat
many kinds of food
to stay healthy.

The food guide pyramid shows the foods you need to stay healthy. The food guide pyramid has six food groups.

Bread is in the grain group. You need 6 to 11 servings from the grain group every day.

10

Peas are in the
vegetable group. You
need three to five servings
of vegetables every day.

Apples are in the
fruit group. You need
two to four servings
of fruit every day.

Milk is in the dairy group. You need two to three servings from the dairy group every day.

Chicken is in the meat and protein group.
You need two to three servings of meat and protein every day.

A cookie is in the fats, oils, and sweets group. You should eat only a small amount of fats, oils, and sweets.

The food guide pyramid helps you make healthy food choices.

Words to Know

dairy—foods made from milk; the dairy group includes cheese, yogurt, and milk.

fruit—the fleshy, juicy part of a plant that people eat

grain—the seed of a cereal plant such as wheat, rice, corn, rye, or barley; foods made from grains include bread, breakfast cereal, rice, and pasta.

healthy—fit and well; exercise and good food choices from the food guide pyramid help keep your body healthy.

meat—the part of an animal that people eat; beef, chicken, and fish are kinds of meat.

protein—a substance found in all plants and animals; meat, eggs, beans, and fish are good sources of protein.

sweet—a food that contains a lot of sugar

vegetable—the part of a plant that people eat

Read More

Bryant-Mole, Karen. *Food.* Picture This! Crystal Lake, Ill.: Rigby, 1997.

Lynn, Sara and Diane James. *What We Eat: A First Look at Food.* Chicago: Worldbook/Two-Can, 1997.

McGinty, Alice B. *Staying Healthy: Eating Right.* The Library of Healthy Living. New York: PowerKids Press, 1997.

Internet Sites

Food Guide Pyramid
http://www.kidshealth.org/kid/food/pyramid.html

Food Pyramid Guide: The Easy Way to Eat Right!
http://www.ganesa.com/food

Nutrition and the Food Pyramid
http://www2.lhric.org/pocantico/
nutrition/nutrition.html

Index/Word List

amount, 19
apples, 13
bread, 9
chicken, 17
choices, 21
cookie, 19
dairy group, 15
eat, 5, 19
fats, oils, and
 sweets group,
 19
food, 5, 7, 21
food groups, 7
food guide
 pyramid, 7, 21
fruit, 13
fruit group, 13
grain group, 9
healthy, 5, 7, 21
meat and protein
 group, 17
milk, 15
peas, 11
servings, 9, 11,
 13, 15, 17
vegetable group,
 11
vegetables, 11

Word Count: 151
Early-Intervention Level: 12

Editorial Credits
Mari C. Schuh, editor; Heather Kindseth, cover designer; Sara A. Sinnard, illustrator;
 Kia Bielke, illustrator; Kimberly Danger, photo researcher

Photo Credits
David F. Clobes, cover, 16
Index Stock Imagery, 1
International Stock/Mimi Cotter, 8
Jean M. Fogle, 10
Mark Turner, 12
Photo Agora, 18
Photo Network/Esbin-Anderson, 4; M. F. Cate, 20
Unicorn Stock Photos/Jean Higgins, 14